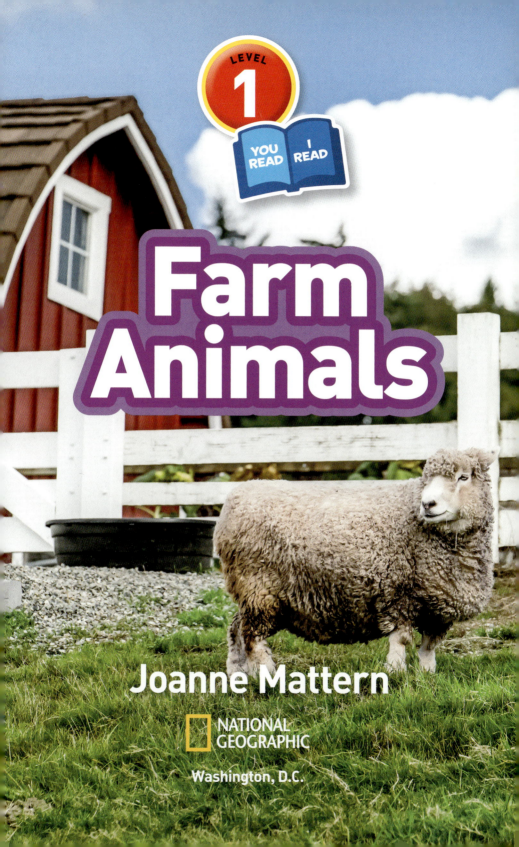

How to Use This Book

Reading together is fun! When older and younger readers share the experience, it opens the door to new learning. As you read together, talk about what you learn.

This side is for a parent, older sibling, or older friend. Before reading each page, take a look at the words and pictures. Talk about what you see. Point out words that might be hard for the younger reader.

This side is for the younger reader.

As you read, look for the bolded words. Talk about them before you read. In each chapter, the bolded words are:
Chapter 1: kinds of farms • Chapter 2: places for animals
Chapter 3: machines on a farm

At the end of each chapter, do the activity together.

Table of Contents

Chapter 1: What's a Farm? ... 4

Your Turn! ... 18

Chapter 2: A Day on the Farm ... 20

Your Turn! ... 34

Chapter 3:
From Animals to Machines ... 36

Your Turn! ... 46

CHAPTER 1

What's a Farm?

 A farm is a place where people produce things. Some of the things are sold. Some are used there on the farm. There are many kinds of farms. Some kinds, like **dairy** farms, have animals. On other types of farms, fruits and vegetables are grown.

 A farmer has cows on a **dairy** farm. Twice a day, the farmer milks the cows. Then the farmer can sell the milk.

On many **poultry** farms, chickens are free range. This means they can wander around a large area to find food.

 Every day on a **poultry** farm, the chickens lay eggs. The farmer collects the eggs and sells them.

 On a **sheep** farm, sheep grow thick wool to stay warm through the winter. In the spring, the farmer shaves the sheep and collects the wool to sell. People buy the wool to make clothes.

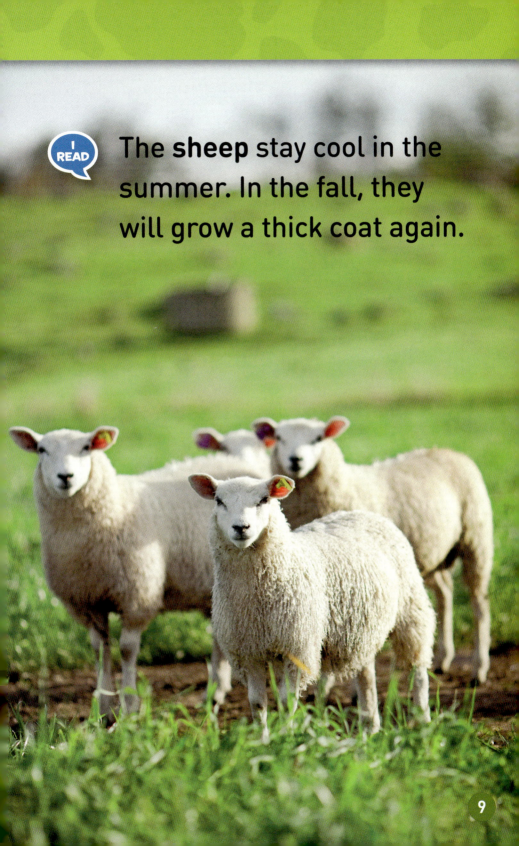

I READ The **sheep** stay cool in the summer. In the fall, they will grow a thick coat again.

Not all farmers raise animals. Some farmers grow crops. Animals eat crops, and people use crops to make food. On a **wheat** farm, fields of wheat are cut down in the fall. Then some parts of the wheat are bundled to sell.

Sometimes crops are used for animal food. These cows eat corn.

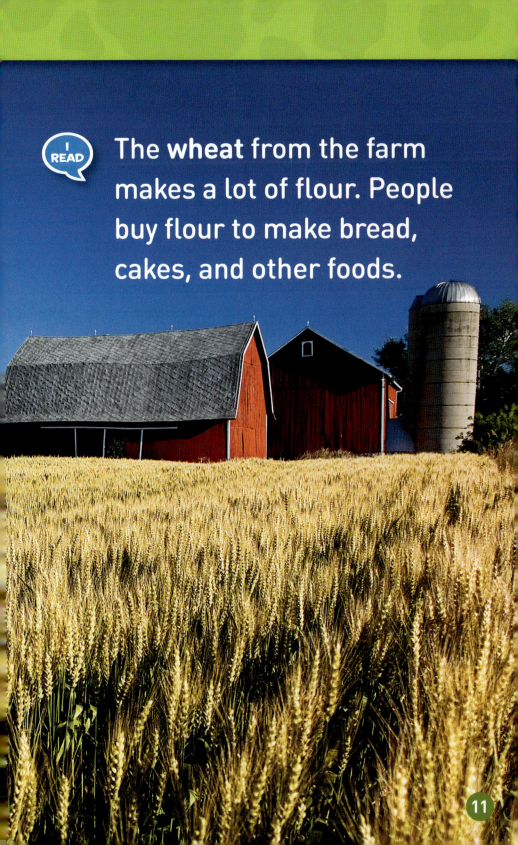

I READ

The **wheat** from the farm makes a lot of flour. People buy flour to make bread, cakes, and other foods.

Other farmers have **orchards**. An apple orchard produces apples every year. The apples are harvested in the fall and sold to make cider and apple pie.

Apples that fall can be a tasty treat for birds, bugs, and horses, too!

Some farmers grow fruit **orchards**. Other farmers grow nut orchards.

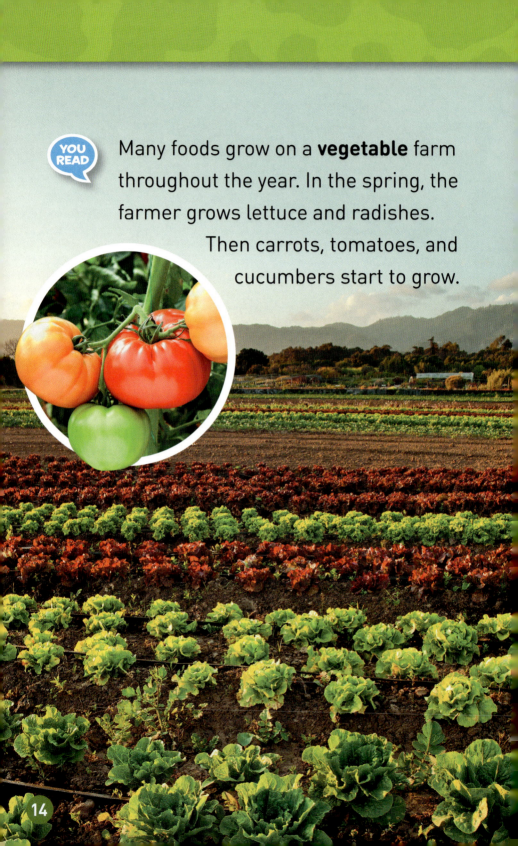

YOU READ

Many foods grow on a **vegetable** farm throughout the year. In the spring, the farmer grows lettuce and radishes. Then carrots, tomatoes, and cucumbers start to grow.

I READ

Other **vegetables** are planted later in the year. Squash and pumpkins grow in the fall.

Rabbits eat carrots from a vegetable farm.

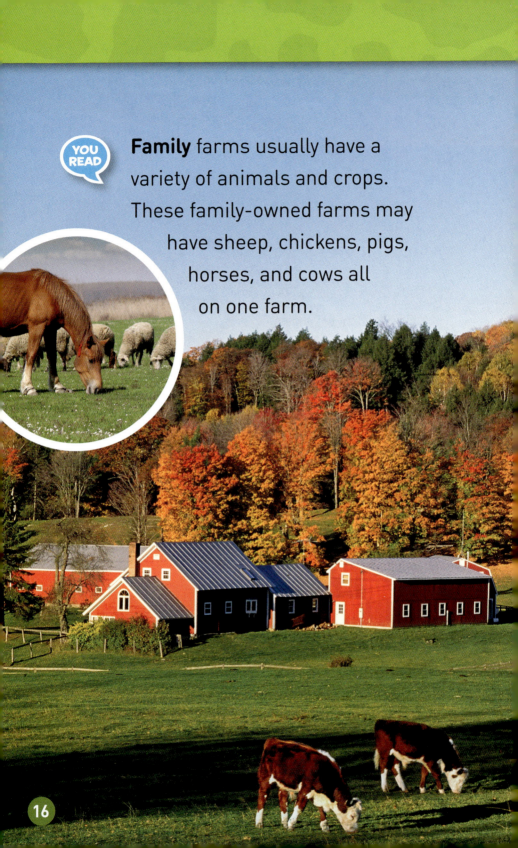

Family farms usually have a variety of animals and crops. These family-owned farms may have sheep, chickens, pigs, horses, and cows all on one farm.

A **family** farm produces and sells many things. One farmer can sell eggs, wool, and meat at a farmers market.

YOUR TURN!

These photos show things that farms produce. Guess what product each photo shows.

ANSWERS (clockwise from top) Page 18: fruit/apples, wool, wheat; Page 19: eggs, milk, vegetables, pumpkins

19

CHAPTER 2

A Day on the Farm

YOU READ

On a family farm, the sun slowly rises on a new summer day. A rooster crows loudly, and the cows stand next to a gate. Soon, the farmer will lead them into a **field**.

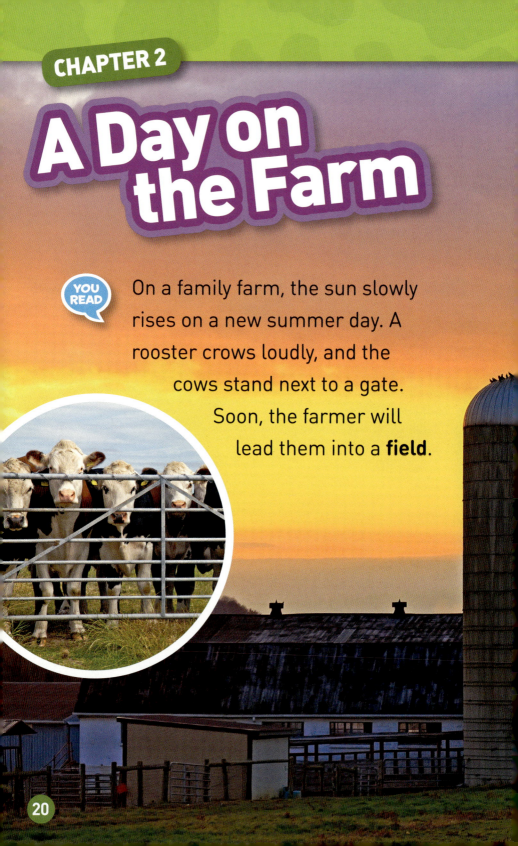

The farmer opens the gate. The cows walk through. The grass in the **field** is green and thick. The cows eat.

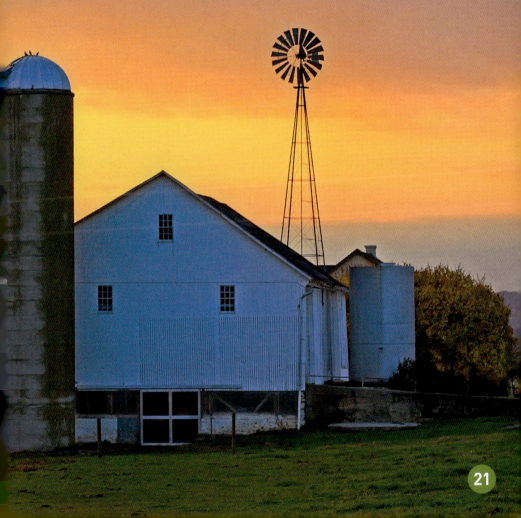

The sun rises higher, and chickens begin to roam around the **yard**. The farmer has scattered grain for them. The chickens are hungry, so they use their beaks to peck and eat.

 Chickens eat other things in the **yard**, too. They use their beaks to dig for worms.

It's noon and the sun is high now. It's hot. The pigs stay in the shade in their **pen**. They drink water from a long trough.

 The pigs roll in the mud in their **pen**. The wet mud cools them.

 It's late afternoon now. In a **pasture** beyond the field, a sheep looks up and runs. A black-and-white dog bounds over the hill. The dog is a border collie. Its job is to herd the sheep to a new place.

 The farmer wants to use the **pasture** for other animals. The dog helps the farmer move the sheep away.

 The sun begins to set, and the animals move again. The horses in the field change direction and trot together toward the **stable**.

The farmer opens the **stable** door. Each horse has its own space inside. The horses will eat and sleep standing up.

It's getting dark now. The chickens get ready to roost in their **coop**. One by one they flutter inside, where it's comfortable and warm.

The chickens look around the **coop**. Soon it will be dark. Then they will sleep.

 It's night on the farm. Cows and sheep snuggle down in the straw and settle in for the night. They lie close together in the **barn** to keep warm.

It's quiet in the **barn** now. All the animals are asleep.

YOUR TURN!

Say where these animals go.

barn

ANSWERS: chicken–coop; horse–stable; pig–pen; cow–barn

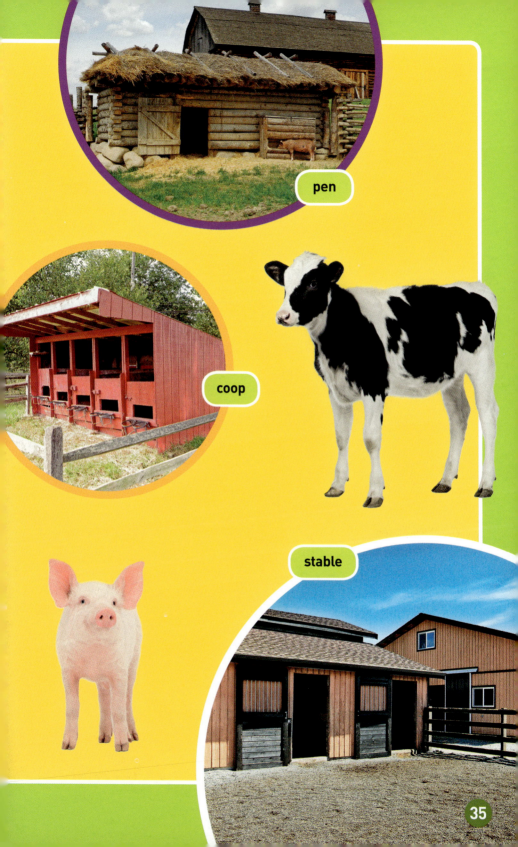

CHAPTER 3
From Animals to Machines

YOU READ

Work on a farm is hard. Animals such as horses, oxen, and mules used to do most of the heavy work. Today farmers often use machines. On a wheat farm in the spring, the farmer uses a **tractor** to pull a smaller machine to the field.

The **tractor** is strong. It pulls the small machine a long way.

 The small machine is called a **plow**. It has many sharp parts that move in a circle. A plow digs deep into the soil, turning it over and over.

Chickens used to do this work. They peck and scratch in the soil to turn it over.

The **plow** gets rid of weeds. Now the soil is ready for seeds.

Next, the farmer uses a machine called a **grain drill**. This machine first digs holes in the soil and then drops seeds through tubes.

The **grain drill** pushes the wheat seeds into the ground. It covers the seeds up. Now the wheat can grow.

wheat

The wheat grows tall through the summer. Finally in the fall, it's ready to be harvested. A farmer uses a **combine** to cut, separate, and clean the wheat. Then the wheat will be processed and sold.

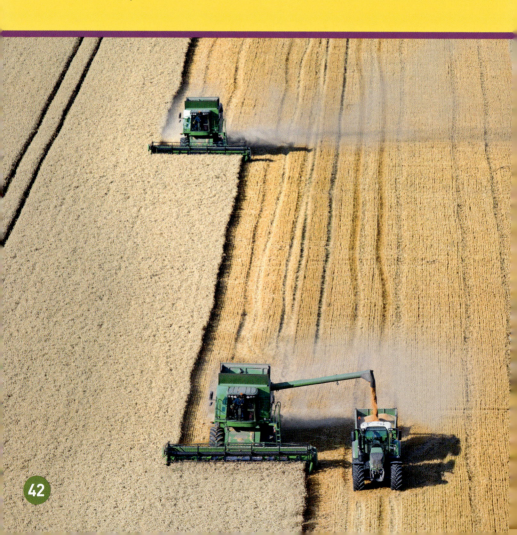

 The **combine** saves the farmer a lot of work. It does three jobs at once.

Not all farmers have big machines. In many places, farmers continue to use **animals** to help them do the hard work.

These **animals** are strong. They do important jobs. The farmer could not run the farm without their help.

YOUR TURN!

Act out what each machine does.

tractor plow

donkey plow

Copyright © 2017 National Geographic Partners, LLC

Published by National Geographic Partners, LLC, Washington, DC, 20036. All rights reserved. Reproduction in whole or in part without written permission of the publisher is prohibited.

NATIONAL GEOGRAPHIC and Yellow Border Design are trademarks of the National Geographic Society, used under license.

Art Director: Amanda Larsen

The publisher and author gratefully acknowledge the expert literacy review by Kimberly Gillow, principal, Milan Area Schools, Michigan.

Library of Congress Cataloging-in-Publication Data

Names: Mattern, Joanne, 1963- author. | National Geographic Society (U.S.)
Title: Farm animals / by Joanne Mattern.
Description: [First edition]. | Washington, DC : National Geographic, [2017]
  | Series: National geographic readers
Identifiers: LCCN 2016039647 (print) | LCCN 2016043530 (ebook) | ISBN
  9781426326875 (pbk. : alk. paper) | ISBN 9781426326882 (hardcover : alk.
  paper) | ISBN 9781426326899 (e-book)
Subjects: LCSH: Livestock--Juvenile literature. | Domestic animals--Juvenile
  literature. | Farm life--Juvenile literature.
Classification: LCC SF75.5 .M38 2017 (print) | LCC SF75.5 (ebook) | DDC
  636.01--dc23
LC record available at https://lccn.loc.gov/2016039647

Photo Credits
Cover, Nate Allred/Shutterstock; Heading, throughout, vectorob/Shutterstock; 1 (CTR), Janet Horton/Alamy Stock Photo; 3 (LO), Byrdyak/Getty Images; 4 (LO), Jenoche/Shutterstock; 5 (UP), Picavet/Getty Images; 5 (LO), Andrey_Kuzmin/Shutterstock; 6 (UP), Fotokostic/Shutterstock; 6 (LO), Tsekhmister/Shutterstock; 7 (UP), D. Hurst/Alamy Stock Photo; 7 (LO), GMEVIPHOTO/Shutterstock; 8 (UP), FlairImages/Getty Images; 8 (LO), Velychko/Shutterstock; 9 (CTR), Sonja Dahlgren/Getty Images; 10-11 (CTR), Image Studios/Getty Images; 10 (LO LE), emholk/Getty Images; 12 (UP), Lya_Cattel/Getty Images; 12 (LO), RusGri/Shutterstock; 13 (CTR), Tierfotoagentur/Alamy Stock Photo; 14 (UP), Dogayusufdokdok/Getty Images; 14 (CTR), Premium UIG/Getty Images; 15 (UP), George Grall/National Geographic Creative; 15 (LO), Photomaster/Shutterstock; 16 (CTR), Gallo Images/Getty Images; 16 (UP), Goce/Getty Images; 17 (LO), Hero Images/Getty Images; 18 (CTR), Brent Winebrenner/Getty Images; 18 (LO), Alex Melnick/Shutterstock; 18 (LO), Alexander Mazurkevich/Shutterstock; 19 (UP), The Len/Shutterstock; 19 (CTR), Louise Heusinkveld/Getty Images; 19 (LO), Premium UIG/Getty Images; 19 (RT), R-J-Seymour/Getty Images; 20 (CTR), Delmas Lehman/Getty Images; 20 (CTR), F_/Getty Images; 22 (LO), Baianliang/Getty Images; 23 (CTR), eurobanks/Shutterstock; 23 (LO), kzww/Shutterstock; 24 (CTR), FLPA/Alamy Stock Photo; 25 (CTR), Jeff Kimball/Kimball Stock; 26 (UP), Kevin Oke/Getty Images; 28 (UP), Jordi Angrill/Getty Images; 29 (LO), blickwinkel/Alamy Stock Photo; 30 (CTR), Goldistocks/Getty Images; 31 (CTR), Shutterjack/Getty Images; 32 (UP), Martin Holste/Getty Images; 33 (CTR), Jupiterimages/Getty Images; 34 (LE), 4nadia/Getty Images; 34 (CTR), Valentina_S/Shutterstock; 34 (CTR), Isselee/Dreamstime; 35 (UP), Peter Carroll/Getty Images; 35 (CTR), Lovesdobermans/Getty Images; 35 (LO), Iriana Shiyan/Getty Images; 35 (CTR), Eric Isselee/Shutterstock; 35 (LO LE), Tsekhmister/Shutterstock; 36 (CTR), Oticki/Getty Images; 36 (CTR), Bettmann/Getty Images; 38 (UP), Rades6/Getty Images; 38 (LO), Matee Nuserm/Shutterstock; 39 (CTR), Design Pics Inc/Alamy Stock Photo; 40 (CTR), smereka/Shutterstock; 41 (LO), Earleliason/Getty Images; 42 (LO), Echo/Getty Images; 43 (UP), Anthony Boccaccio/Getty Images; 44-45 (CTR), Roberto Fumagalli/Alamy Stock Photo; 46 (LO), Matthew Williams-Ellis/Getty Images; 46 (CTR), Dieter Meyrl/Getty Images; 47 (UP), Edwin Remsberg/Getty Images; 47 (LO), Oticki/Getty Images

**National Geographic supports K–12 educators with ELA Common Core Resources.
Visit natgeoed.org/commoncore for more information.**

Printed in the United States of America
16/WOR/1